HEALT RECIPES FOR BEGINNERS

C000154169

QUICK & EASY

Paola Clifford

Welcome!

To this new series of book, inspired by all the recipes I know thanks to my great passion: *cooking!*

"You really know what you are eating if you make it yourself"

In this book you will find many different ideas for your dishes, with ingredients from all around the world, with a Gourmet touch!

Thanks to these cookbooks you can develop your cooking skills for any kind of meal, as you'll find recipes for:

★ salads
★ sides
★ lunch
★ dinner
★ Desserts

And much more...

Whether your favourite dish is French fries, muffins, chicken tenders or grilled vegetables, with this series of books you will learn how to do it with a better-looking touch!

Don't forget that this books have also low fat recipes with healthy ingredients to *keep you fit and have a healthier meal plan!*

Remember that having a wide variety of ingredients and foods in your diet have many benefits for you, that's why you will find ingredients from:

★ Asia
★ Russia
★ America
★ Europe

And much more...

Since I started to pay more attention on the decision of the ingredients and how to plate a dish, I enjoy cooking a lot more! That's why I made this cookbook for all of you that want to develop your cooking skills and start eating healthier!

 I hope you will enjoy this book! Don't forget to check out the other ones from the collection, and enjoy your time in the kitchen!

HEALTHY RECIPES
FOR BEGINNERS

QUICK AND EASY

LEARN HOW TO MIX DIFFERENT INGREDIENTS AND SPICES TO
CREATE DELICIOUS DISHES AND BUILD A COMPLETE MEAL PLAN!
THIS COOKBOOK INCLUDES QUICK-AND-EASY RECIPES TO
PREPARE ON A DAILY BASIS, FOR AN EFFECTIVE DIET AND A
HEALTHIER LIFESTYLE FOR YOUR 2021

Paola Clifford

HEALTHY RECIPES FOR BEGINNERS: APPETIZERS

Learn how to mix different ingredients and spices to create delicious dishes and build a complete meal plan! This cookbook includes quick recipes to prepare on a daily basis, for an effective diet and a healthier lifestyle!

HEALTHY RECIPES FOR BEGINNERS: SIDES

Learn how to mix different ingredients and spices to create delicious dishes and build a complete meal plan! This cookbook includes quick recipes to prepare on a daily basis, for an effective diet and a healthier lifestyle!

HEALTHY RECIPES FOR BEGINNERS: QUICK AND EASY

Learn how to mix different ingredients and spices to create delicious dishes and build a complete meal plan! This cookbook includes quick-and-easy recipes to prepare on a daily basis, for an effective diet and a Healthier lifestyle for your 2021!

HEALTHY RECIPES FOR BEGINNERS: LUNCH

Learn how to mix different ingredients and spices to create delicious dishes and build a complete meal plan! This cookbook includes quick recipes to prepare on a daily basis, for an effective diet and a healthier lifestyle!

HEALTHY RECIPES FOR BEGINNERS: DESSERTS

Learn how to mix different ingredients and fruit to create delicious desserts and build a complete meal plan! This cookbook includes quick and easy recipes for both adults and kids, from the Mediterranean and other well-known diets!

HEALTHY RECIPES FOR BEGINNERS: TOP 50

Learn how to mix different ingredients to create Delicious meals and build a complete meal plan for your diet! This cookbook includes quick-and-easy recipes for all your family. Amaze your friends with your cooking skills!

HEALTHY RECIPES FOR BEGINNERS: SALADS

Lose weight by eating well! Learn how to mix different ingredients and fruit to create delicious salads and build a complete meal plan! This cookbook includes quick and easy recipes for both adults and kids, from the mediterranean and other well-known diets!

HEALTHY RECIPES FOR BEGINNERS: DINNER

Learn how to mix different ingredients and spices to create delicious dishes and build a complete meal plan! This cookbook includes quick and easy recipes to prepare on a daily basis, for an effective diet and a healthier lifestyle!

SALADS AND LUNCH MEAL PREP

2 books in 1: Healthy salad and lunch recipes for beginners. Lose weight by eating well! This cookbook contains some of the best low-fat recipes that also ideal for weight loss and body-healing routines. Improve your cooking skills with the right book!

COMPLETE DINNER COOKBOOK

This boundle contains 3 recipe books in 1: healthy dinner, desserts and sides recipes for beginner.

Learn how to use different ingredients, herbs, spices and plants to cook delicious dishes for your complete meal plan.

Table of Contents

QUICK & EASY,
SMART & HEALTHY

Polenta Fries

Serving: 8

Ingredients

- 2 cups whole milk

- 1 quart chicken stock

- 2 tablespoons butter

- 3 1/4 cups dry polenta

- 3 ounces Parmesan cheese

- 1/4 cup chopped fresh parsley

- salt and pepper to taste

- 1 quart vegetable oil for frying

Direction

- Mix together butter, chicken stock and milk in a big saucepan; bring it to a rolling boil. Whisk in polenta gently. Reduce heat to medium-low, and keep cooking and mixing till polenta pull away from side of pan. Add parsley and cheese, and put in pepper and salt to taste. On a cookie sheet, scatter polenta equally, and chill till cold.

- Move polenta to a chopping board, slice into 3/4× 3/4×3 1/2-inch sticks.

- In deep-fryer, heat oil to 185°C or 365°F. In batches, fry polenta sticks till crispy. Drain by putting them on dry paper towels.

Nutrition Information

- Calories: 493 calories;

- Sodium: 1436

- Total Carbohydrate: 53.7

- Cholesterol: 29

- Protein: 15.1

- Total Fat: 24.6

Polenta And Vegetable Casserole

Serving: 6

Ingredients

- 1 (16 ounce) tube polenta, cut into 1/2 inch slices

- 1 (16 ounce) can black beans

- 1 (15 ounce) can kidney beans

- 1 (10 ounce) can whole kernel corn

- 1 onion, chopped

- 1 green bell pepper, chopped

- 1 small eggplant, peeled and cubed

- 6 fresh mushrooms, chopped

- 1 (1.27 ounce) packet dry fajita seasoning

- 1 (8 ounce) jar salsa

- 1 cup shredded mozzarella cheese
- 1/3 cup black olives

Direction

Preheat the oven to 175 °C or 350 °F. Lightly grease a baking dish of 9x13 inches square with oil.

In a skillet, heat oil over medium heat. In hot oil, cook and mix mushrooms, eggplant, green pepper and onion till tender. Blend in the fajita seasoning.

Line slices of polenta on prepped baking dish. Evenly scatter corn and beans on top of polenta, and then scatter the onion mixture on top of the beans. Put black olives, mozzarella cheese and salsa on top.

Bake for 20 minutes till heated through.

Nutrition Information

- Calories: 329 calories;
- Sodium: 1633
- Total Carbohydrate: 57.5
- Cholesterol: 12

- Protein: 17.8

- Total Fat: 5

Portabella Mushroom Dressing

Serving: 8

Ingredients

4 stalks celery

1 onion, chopped

2 large portobello mushrooms, sliced

3 fresh shiitake mushrooms, stemmed and sliced

8 crimini mushrooms, sliced

2 cloves garlic, minced

1 (12 ounce) package dry bread stuffing mix with seasoning packet reserved

3 (14.5 ounce) cans chicken broth

Direction

- Preheat the oven to 175°C or 350°F.

- Cook and mix garlic, mushrooms, onion and celery for 3 minutes in a skillet. Mix in 1 can of chicken broth and cook till vegetables are soft. With bread crumb stuffing, mix mushroom mixture. Put packet of seasoning on top of dressing mixture and coat by tossing.

- Heat the rest of chicken broth in a 2-quart saucepan till hot. Put broth on top of mixture. Mix thoroughly.

- Into a 2-quart casserole dish, put the stuffing and allow to bake for 30 to 40 minutes.

Nutrition Information

- Calories: 188 calories;

- Total Fat: 1.5

- Sodium: 694

- Total Carbohydrate: 36.5

- Cholesterol: 1

- Protein: 6.6

Potato Latkes I

Serving: 6

Ingredients

- 2 cups peeled and shredded potatoes

- 1 tablespoon grated onion

- 3 eggs, beaten

- 2 tablespoons all-purpose flour

- 1 1/2 teaspoons salt

- 1/2 cup peanut oil for frying

Direction

- In a cheesecloth, put potatoes and squeeze, squeezing out as much moisture as there is.

- Mix the salt, flour, eggs, onion and potatoes together in a medium bowl.

- In a big heavy-bottomed skillet, heat oil over medium-high heat till hot. Into the hot oil, put heaping spoonfuls of potato mixture, patting them down to create a quarter to half-inch thick patties. Brown on 1 side, flip and brown on another side. Drain on paper towels. Serve while hot.

Nutrition Information

- Calories: 102 calories;

- Total Fat: 4.4

- Sodium: 620

- Total Carbohydrate: 11.3

- Cholesterol: 93

- Protein: 4.5

Potato Latkes II

Serving: 6

Ingredients

2 cups potato, cubed

3 Yukon Gold potatoes, peeled and shredded

1 onion, shredded

2 eggs

3 tablespoons matzo meal

1 teaspoon kosher salt

6 tablespoons vegetable oil

Direction

- Boil a big pot of salted water. Put in potatoes and cook for 15 minutes till soft yet firm. Drain, cool and mash.

- Combine onion, mashed potatoes and shredded Yukon Gold potatoes in a medium bowl. Put in salt, matzo meal and eggs; combine thoroughly.

- Test the consistency of dough; mixture should hold together without being sticky. In case it sticks to hands, put in additional matzo meal till dough is not sticky anymore.

- Heat sufficient margarine, butter or oil in a big skillet over medium heat to fill skillet by a quarter inch.

- Once hot, drop mixture by heaping tablespoon into oil; flatten using a spatula and cook each side till golden brown. Serve.

Nutrition Information

- Calories: 252 calories;
- Total Fat: 15.8
- Sodium: 351
- Total Carbohydrate: 23.8
- Cholesterol: 62
- Protein: 4.9

Prosciutto Wrapped Asparagus

Serving: 4

Ingredients

1/2 pound prosciutto, sliced

1/2 (8 ounce) package Neufchatel cheese, softened

12 spears fresh asparagus, trimmed

Direction

Preheat the oven to 230 °C or 450 °F.

Scatter Neufchatel cheese on slices of prosciutto. Wrap 2 or 3 asparagus spears in the slices. On a medium baking sheet, set wrapped spears in 1 layer.

In the prepped oven, bake for 15 minutes, till asparagus is soft.

Nutrition Information

Calories: 292 calories;

Total Carbohydrate: 2.7

Cholesterol: 71

Protein: 14.8

Total Fat: 24.6

Sodium: 1210

Quick And Easy Indian Style Okra

Serving: 6

Ingredients

1/3 cup vegetable oil

1/4 teaspoon mustard seed

1 pinch asafoetida powder

1 medium onion, thinly sliced

1 clove garlic, peeled and sliced

1/4 teaspoon cumin seed

1/8 teaspoon ground turmeric

1 large tomato, chopped

1 (16 ounce) package frozen sliced okra

1/4 teaspoon chili powder

1 teaspoon amchoor

salt to taste

Direction

In medium skillet, heat oil on medium heat. Cook mustard seed till it starts to crackle. Mix asafetida in. Lower heat to low; mix turmeric, cumin seed, garlic and onion in. Mix and cook for about 5 minutes till onion is tender.

Mix okra and tomato into mixture. Mix salt, amchoor and chili powder in slowly. Mix and cook till okra is tender yet firm for about 10 minutes.

Nutrition Information

Calories: 146 calories;

Cholesterol: 0

Protein: 1.8

Total Fat: 12.5

Sodium: 6

Total Carbohydrate: 8.6

Raisin Farfel Kugel

Serving: 6

Ingredients

2 cups farfel

6 eggs, beaten

1/2 cup raisins

1/2 teaspoon salt

1 cup white sugar

2 tablespoons ground cinnamon

4 tablespoons butter

Direction

Set oven to 350 degrees F (175 degrees C) and grease a baking dish of 8x8 inches in size.

Soak the farfel for 10 minutes in water, then drain.

Beat eggs into the farfel in a bowl and allow to stand for 10 minutes. Stir in butter, cinnamon, sugar, salt, and raisins. Move the mixture to the prepared baking dish.

Bake in the oven for 50-60 minutes at 350 degrees F or 175 degrees C.

Nutrition Information

Calories: 412 calories;

Sodium: 320

Total Carbohydrate: 66.5

Cholesterol: 206

Protein: 9.3

Total Fat: 13.1

Red Bell Pepper Coulis

Serving: 4

Ingredients

1 tablespoon olive oil

2 red bell peppers, seeded and chopped

2 shallots, chopped

1/2 cup white wine

1/2 cup chicken broth

1/2 cup sour cream

Direction

In a skillet over medium heat, heat the olive oil. Put shallots and red bell peppers; sauté till tender. Mix in chicken broth and white wine, and let simmer over low heat till reduced by 1/2.

Once mixture is reduced, mix in the sour cream, and to a blender, put the mixture. Puree till smooth. Reheat prior serving if needed.

Nutrition Information

Calories: 153 calories;

Total Fat: 9.6

Sodium: 22

Total Carbohydrate: 9.8

Cholesterol: 13

Protein: 2.1

Red Chard And Caramelized Onions

Serving: 4

Ingredients

1 large yellow onion, chopped

2 tablespoons olive oil

1 teaspoon brown sugar

1 bunch red Swiss chard, rinsed and chopped

1/4 cup kalamata olives

2 tablespoons capers

1/2 teaspoon coarse sea salt, or to taste

freshly ground black pepper to taste

1 lemon, juiced

Direction

- On medium-high heat, cook onions in a cast iron pan with olive oil until they start to brown; mix in brown sugar. Keep on cooking for a couple of minutes.

- Mix in olives and chard once the onions are tender and brown; cook until the chard is a bit wilted. Mix in salt and capers; continue to cook for about 3mins until the chard is wilted completely. Sprinkle black pepper to season; squeeze lemon on top.

Nutrition Information

- Calories: 118 calories;

- Sodium: 608

- Total Carbohydrate: 8.9

- Cholesterol: 0

- Protein: 1.7

- Total Fat: 9.2

Red Swiss Chard With Pine Nuts And Prosciutto

Serving: 4

Ingredients

- 2 teaspoons olive oil

- 1/4 cup pine nuts

- 2 cloves garlic, minced

- 8 cups chopped red Swiss chard

- salt and ground black pepper to taste

- 1/4 pound sliced prosciutto, chopped

Direction

- On medium heat, heat olive oil in a big pan; add pine nuts. Cook and stir for about 2mins until light golden brown. Look after the cooking pine nuts carefully since they easily burn. Mix in garlic, cook for about a minute more while stirring regularly until aromatic.

- Add the Swiss chard, cook and stir for 3-5mins until wilted; sprinkle black pepper and salt to season. Gently mix in chopped prosciutto; cook and stir just until the prosciutto is hot. Serve.

Nutrition Information

- Calories: 190 calories;

- Protein: 8.9

- Total Fat: 15.8

- Sodium: 703

- Total Carbohydrate: 4.4

- Cholesterol: 25

Roasted Asparagus With Shallots

Serving: 4

Ingredients

- 2 bunches fresh asparagus spears, trimmed

- 4 medium shallots, thinly sliced

- 4 tablespoons extra-virgin olive oil

- 3 tablespoons red wine vinegar, divided

- salt and pepper to taste

Direction

- Preheat an oven to 200°C or 400°F.

- In a big bowl, put the shallots and asparagus; put 2 tablespoons of vinegar and the olive oil on top of them. Put pepper and salt to season, then evenly coat by tossing. On a baking sheet, scatter asparagus spears in 1 layer.

- In the preheated oven, let bake for 20 minutes, or till bright green and soft. Approximately half way through, roll the spears over by shaking the pan for even cooking. Take off from oven, sprinkle the rest of the vinegar on asparagus. Coat by lightly tossing; serve right away.

Nutrition Information

- Calories: 206 calories;

- Total Carbohydrate: 18

- Cholesterol: 0

- Protein: 6.2

- Total Fat: 13.8

- Sodium: 11

Roasted Beets And Sauteed Beet Greens

Serving: 4

Ingredients

- 1 bunch beets with
- greens
- 1/4 cup olive oil, divided
- 2 cloves garlic, minced
- 2 tablespoons chopped onion (optional)
- salt and pepper to taste
- 1 tablespoon red wine vinegar (optional)

Direction

- Heat the oven to 350 degrees F or 175 degrees C. Wash beets well with the skins on and remove the greens. Rinse greens and remove the large stems, then put aside. In a small roasting pan or baking dish, place the beets and toss with 2 tablespoons olive oil. You can peel the beets if desired, but it is easier after roasting them.

- Bake, covered, for 45-60 minutes until a knife slides easily through the biggest beet.

- When roasting is almost done, use a skillet to heat the remaining 2 tablespoons olive oil over medium-low heat. Add the onion and garlic, then cook for 1 minute. Tear beet greens into 2-3 inch pieces, and add to the skillet. Cook while stirring until the greens soften and wilt, then season with pepper and salt. Serve the greens as they are and the roasted beets sliced with either butter-pepper-salt or red wine vinegar.

Nutrition Information

- Calories: 204 calories;

- Total Carbohydrate: 18

- Cholesterol: 0

- Protein: 5.3

- Total Fat: 13.9

- Sodium: 442

Roasted Garlic Mashed Potatoes

Serving: 8

Ingredients

- 6 cloves garlic, peeled

- 1/4 cup olive oil

- 7 baking potatoes, peeled and cubed

- 1/2 cup milk

- 1/4 cup grated Parmesan cheese

- 2 tablespoons butter

- 1/2 teaspoon salt

- 1/4 teaspoon ground black pepper

Direction

- Heat the oven beforehand to 175 °C or 350 °F.

- Put garlic cloves in small baking dish then drizzle olive oil on top. Cover and bake until they become golden brown, about 45 minutes.

- Bring big pot with lightly salted water to a boil. Put in potatoes then cook until they become tender yet still firm. Drain and put them in a big mixing bowl.

- In the bowl with the potatoes, put butter, parmesan cheese, milk and roasted garlic. Use pepper and salt to season. Use an electric mixer to beat to desired consistency.

Nutrition Information

- Calories: 251 calories;

- Total Fat: 10.8

- Sodium: 222

- Total Carbohydrate: 34.2

- Cholesterol: 11

- Protein: 5.4

Roasted Garlic Sweet Potatoes

Serving: 8

Ingredients

- 4 sweet potatoes

- 2 heads garlic

- 2 tablespoons olive oil

- 2 tablespoons butter (at room temperature)

- 3/4 cup light sour cream

- 1/2 cup reduced-fat cream cheese

- 1/2 teaspoon cayenne pepper (optional)

- salt and pepper to taste

Direction

- Preheat the oven to 200°C or 400°F.

- Using the tip of a paring knife or a fork, puncture the sweet potatoes; reserve. Remove the top of heads of garlic to reveal the cloves, clipping approximately quarter an inch off of top of every clove. You may have to clip individual cloves together with the sides of every head. With olive oil, brush cut cloves, then into a piece of aluminum foil, place every head.

- Directly put garlic cloves and sweet potatoes on oven racks. Let bake for an hour, taking off sweet potatoes when they have softened, and taking off garlic heads when they are tender and browned nicely.

- Remove sweet potatoes skin, and put into a mixing bowl. Into the bowl, squeeze each garlic cloves, then put cayenne pepper, cream cheese, sour cream and butter. Crush till smooth, then season with pepper and salt to taste. Into a 1 1/2-quart baking dish, scoop the mashed potatoes, and put back into the oven for approximately 15 minutes to rewarm.

Nutrition Information

- Calories: 200 calories;

- Total Fat: 11.9

- Sodium: 135

- Total Carbohydrate: 19.9

- Cholesterol: 25

- Protein: 4.3

Roasted Potatoes With Tomatoes, Basil, And Garlic

Serving: 8 |

Ingredients

- 2 pounds red potatoes, chopped

- 1 1/2 cups chopped fresh tomatoes

- 3/4 cup fresh basil, chopped

- 3 cloves garlic, pressed

- 3 tablespoons extra virgin olive oil

- 1 teaspoon chopped fresh rosemary

Direction

- Preheat the oven to 200°C or 400°F.

- Toss garlic, basil, tomatoes and potatoes with olive oil in the prepped baking dish. Scatter rosemary on top.

- In the prepped oven, bake for 20 minutes to half an hour, flipping from time to time, till soft.

Roasted White Asparagus With Herbes De Provence

Serving: 4

Ingredients

- 1 bunch white asparagus

- 2 tablespoons olive oil

- 1 1/2 teaspoons herbes de Provence

- 1/4 teaspoon salt

- 1/8 teaspoon ground black pepper

Direction

- Preheat the oven to 200 °C or 400 °F.

- Trim 1 1/2 inches off the bottom of every asparagus stalk. Set flat on a chopping board and remove skin. Move to a casserole dish and brush with olive oil. Scatter black pepper, salt and herbes de Provence on top of asparagus.

- In the prepped oven, roast for 20 minutes till slightly browned.

Nutrition Information

- Calories: 83 calories;
- Total Carbohydrate: 4.4
- Cholesterol: 0
- Protein: 2.5
- Total Fat: 6.9
- Sodium: 148

Roasted Wild Mushrooms And Potatoes

Serving: 4

Ingredients

- 2 pounds new potatoes (such as Yukon Gold), halved

- 2 tablespoons olive oil, or more if needed

- salt to taste

- 1 teaspoon olive oil

- 2 ounces pancetta, chopped

- 1/4 pound king trumpet mushrooms, cut into chunks

- 1/4 pound chanterelle mushrooms, cut into chunks

- 1/4 pound nameko mushrooms, trimmed

Root Vegetables Baked In Pesto Sauce

Serving: 4

Ingredients

- 2 large potatoes, peeled and sliced

- 1 large yam

- 4 carrots, peeled and sliced

- 2 large onion, sliced

- 5 sprigs fresh dill weed

- 1 bunch fresh parsley

- 7 cloves garlic, peeled

- 6 leaves fresh basil

- 3 tablespoons olive oil

Direction

- Preheat the oven to 200°C or 400°F.

- In a 2-quart casserole dish, put the vegetables.

- Mix olive oil, basil, garlic, parsley and dill, in a food processor or blender; process into a smooth paste. Put on top of vegetables. Use aluminum foil to cover the dish.

- In the prepped oven, bake for 40 minutes, or till vegetables are soft.

Nutrition Information

- Calories: 304 calories;

- Total Carbohydrate: 50.4

- Cholesterol: 0

- Protein: 5.5

- Total Fat: 10.6

- Sodium: 52

Saffron Mash Potatoes

Serving: 4

Ingredients

5 cups chicken stock

1 pound Yukon Gold potatoes

1 clove garlic, minced

1 teaspoon saffron threads, crushed

1/2 cup milk

2 tablespoons olive oil

salt and ground black pepper to taste

Direction

- In a big pot, boil saffron, garlic, potatoes and chicken stock; put cover and allow to simmer for about 20 minutes till potatoes are soft.

- Let potatoes drain and put back to pot; set aside cooking stock for other use, if preferred.

- Put black pepper, salt, olive oil and milk to potatoes.

- Using a potato masher, crush potatoes till smooth.

Nutrition Information

- Calories: 180 calories;

- Total Fat: 8.2

- Sodium: 877

- Total Carbohydrate: 23.5

- Cholesterol: 3

- Protein: 4.2

Saffron Rice

Serving: 5

Ingredients

- 2 cups uncooked long-grain rice
- 3/4 teaspoon crushed saffron threads
- 4 tablespoons butter
- 6 whole cardamom seeds
- 4 whole cloves
- 3 cinnamon sticks
- 1 onion, chopped
- 3 cups boiling vegetable broth
- 1 teaspoon salt

Direction

Cover rice with cold water and put aside to submerge for half an hour.

Submerge saffron threads in 2 tablespoons boiling water.

In a big saucepan, melt butter over medium heat; put in cinnamon, cloves and cardamom, and fry for 2 minutes, mixing from time to time. Mix in onion and sauté, mixing from time to time, till golden brown. Mix in rice, turn heat down to low and simmer for 5 minutes, mixing continuously.

Put in boiling broth and mix in saffron and salt.

Put on a cover and cook for 40 minutes till all liquid is soaked up and rice is cooked.

Nutrition Information

Calories: 404 calories;

Sodium: 812

Total Carbohydrate: 69.5

Cholesterol: 24

Protein: 7.1

Total Fat: 10.2

Sauteed Portobellos And Spinach

Serving: 4

Ingredients

3 tablespoons butter

2 large portobello mushrooms, sliced

1 (10 ounce) package frozen chopped spinach, thawed and drained

1/4 teaspoon dried basil

1/4 teaspoon salt

1/4 teaspoon black pepper

1 clove garlic, chopped

2 tablespoons dry red wine

1/4 cup grated Parmesan cheese

Direction

In a big sauté pan or skillet, liquify the butter over medium heat. Sauté garlic, pepper, salt, basil, spinach and mushrooms till spinach is heated through and mushrooms are soft.

Put in wine and lower the heat to low; let simmer for a minute. Mix in the Parmesan cheese, serve.

Nutrition Information

Calories: 146 calories;

Sodium: 359

Total Carbohydrate: 6.6

Cholesterol: 28

Protein: 6.6

Total Fat: 11

Savory Baby Bok Choy

Serving: 4

Ingredients

3 tablespoons butter

1 clove garlic, smashed

1 bay leaf

2 cups chicken stock

1 cup white wine

1 pound baby bok choy, trimmed and sliced in half lengthwise

Direction

- On medium heat in a big skillet, melt butter. Add the garlic and bay leaf; cook and mix it until the garlic gets slightly brown for around 5 minutes. Mix in the white wine and chicken stock then up the heat so it boils. Stir often and cook sauce for about 15 minutes until the amount gets reduced to about a cup. Take out the bay leaf and place in the halved bok choy leaves with the cut sides facing down in the sauce. Turn the heat down to a simmer and cook it until soft for around 10 minutes. Serve with some of the sauce spooned on the bok choy.

Nutrition Information

- Calories: 149 calories;

- Protein: 2.2

- Total Fat: 9.2

- Sodium: 481

- Total Carbohydrate: 4.9

- Cholesterol: 23

Savory Oat Risotto

Serving: 4

Ingredients

3 cups chicken stock

1 bunch spring onions, chopped, or more to taste

5 tablespoons butter, divided

1/2 bunch spring garlic, minced, or more to taste

2 cups steel-cut oats

sea salt and freshly ground black pepper to taste

1/3 cup white wine

1/2 cup grated Parmigiano-Reggiano cheese

Direction

In a small saucepan over medium heat, heat the chicken stock for about 5 minutes till simmering. Take off from heat and put cover to retain warmth.

Gather 2 tablespoons of spring onion tops and set aside.

In a big skillet over medium heat, heat 2 tablespoons of butter till melted. Put the rest of the spring onions to skillet; cook and mix for about a minute till wilted. Put the spring garlic; cook for 2 to 3 minutes, mixing from time to time, till tender.

Into the skillet, mix oats for half a minute. Put 2 tablespoons of butter; cook and mix for about 2 minutes till oats are toasted. Put pepper and salt to season. Add in wine; cook and mix for about 3 minutes till wine has vaporized.

Into the skillet, scoop enough chicken stock to soak oats; let cook for about 3 minutes, mixing frequently, till stock is almost soaked in. Repeat with the rest of the stock for about 24 minutes, mixing frequently till every addition is almost soaked in prior putting additional, till oats are creamy and soft. Mix in leftover spring onion tops and cook for about a minute.

Turn heat to low. Mix in Parmigiano-Reggiano cheese and leftover 1 tablespoon butter for a minute, till melted. Put pepper and salt to season.

Nutrition Information

Calories: 552 calories;

Sodium: 872

Total Carbohydrate: 68.7

Cholesterol: 48

Protein: 16.4

Total Fat: 23

Simple Fried Morel Mushrooms

Serving: 4

Ingredients

- 1 pound fresh morel mushrooms - dirt gently brushed off and mushrooms halved lengthwise

- 1 cup all-purpose flour

- 1 cup vegetable shortening

- salt to taste

Direction

- In a big bowl, cover halved morel mushrooms in cold, lightly salted water. Keep in fridge to loosen dirt for 5 minutes. Pour salted water off. Rinse. Repeat 2 times. The mushroom crevices could have insects or tiny stones. Rinse mushrooms thoroughly one last time. Drain mushrooms on paper towels.

- In a shallow bowl, put flour.

- In a big skillet, heat vegetable shortening until very hot.

- Roll the mushrooms into flour. Tap excess off. Lay mushrooms gently in hot shortening.

- Pan Fry for 5-8 minutes until flour coating is crisp and its golden brown, turning often. On paper towels, drain morels. Use salt to taste.

Nutrition Information

- Calories: 185 calories;

- Total Carbohydrate: 29.2

- Cholesterol: 0

- Protein: 5.9

- Total Fat: 5.3

- Sodium: 39

Smoked Bacon And Irish Cheese Mash

Serving: 8

Ingredients

- 15 potatoes, peeled

- 1 teaspoon vegetable oil

- 10 slices smoked streaky bacon, cut into small pieces

- 1/2 (8 ounce) round Camembert cheese (such as Cooleeney Irish Camembert)

- 2 ounces grated white Cheddar cheese

- 1 spring onion, thinly sliced

- 1/2 cup light cream, divided

- 2 tablespoons butter

- salt and cracked black pepper to taste

Direction

- In a pot of cold water, put the potatoes. Put cover and place over high heat; boil for 20 minutes till easily pricked using a fork. Drain thoroughly and cover for 10 minutes using a clean dish towel.

- Preheat the oven to 200°C or 400°F.

- In a big skillet, heat oil over medium heat. Let cook and mix bacon for 5 to 8 minutes till very crispy. Allow to drain on paper towels.

- In a blender, put the bacon; process into small pieces.

- Break the Camembert cheese into tiny lumps; in a bowl, mix along with spring onion and Cheddar cheese.

- Crush potatoes till smooth. Mix butter, half of the cream, Camembert cheese mixture and bacon into the crushed potatoes. Put pepper and salt to season.

- In a baking dish, scatter crushed potato mixture. Put the rest of the cream over. Prick in few places using a fork.

- In the preheated oven, bake for about 15 minutes till top begins to brown.

Nutrition Information

Calories: 472 calories;

Sodium: 493

Total Carbohydrate: 70.2

Cholesterol: 38

Protein: 17

Total Fat: 14.4

Spaetzle

Serving: 4

Ingredients

- 4 cups all-purpose flour
- 5 eggs
- 1 teaspoon salt
- 3/4 cup water

Direction

- Combine salt, eggs, and flour in a big bowl. Add a little bit of water at a time until forming a soft dough.

- In a big pot, boil 2 quarts water and squeeze out the dough into the water by pressing through a large-holed colander or using a fruit/noodle press. Once the noodles float up, about 3 - 4 minutes, they are done. Serve this as a side or a main dish.

Nutrition Information

- Calories: 544 calories;

- Cholesterol: 231

- Protein: 20.7

- Total Fat: 7.4

- Sodium: 769

- Total Carbohydrate: 95.9

Spiced Eggplant Indian Style

Serving: 4

Ingredients

- 2 1/2 pounds eggplant

- 2/3 cup clarified butter

- 1 cup chopped onions

- 4 large ripe tomatoes, chopped

- 4 teaspoons crushed coriander seed

Direction

Preheat the oven to 165°C or 325°F.

Slice eggplant(s) in half and let bake for 20 minutes, or till soft. Mash eggplant with a pastry blender or potato masher.

In a medium skillet, heat clarified butter over medium heat; sauté the onions till translucent. Mix in eggplant and tomatoes; let cook, mixing, till liquid steams off. Take off from the heat and scatter coriander on top.

Nutrition Information

- Calories: 533 calories;

- Total Fat: 39.7

- Sodium: 839

- Total Carbohydrate: 44.5

- Cholesterol: 87

- Protein: 7.1

Spicy Maple Roasted Delicata Squash

Serving: 1

Ingredients

- 1 delicata squash - halved, seeded, and sliced into 1/2-inch half-moons
- 1 red Fresno chile pepper, sliced very thinly
- 2 tablespoons maple syrup
- 1 teaspoon olive oil
- salt to taste
- ground black pepper to taste

Direction

- Preheat an oven to 220 °C or 425 °F.
- In a bowl, mix pepper, salt, olive oil, maple syrup, Fresno chile and squash together. Put into a baking sheet.

- In the prepped oven, bake for 25 minutes till soft, tossing halfway through.

Nutrition Information

- Calories: 165 calories;

- Sodium: 160

- Total Carbohydrate: 31.3

- Cholesterol: 0

- Protein: 0.5

- Total Fat: 5

Spicy Pakistani Zucchini

Serving: 5

Ingredients

- 1/4 cup cooking oil

- 1 onion, thinly sliced

- 6 zucchini - peeled, seeded and cut into semicircles

- 1/2 teaspoon salt

- 2 cups water

- 2 teaspoons chili powder

- 1/2 teaspoon ground turmeric

- 1/2 teaspoon garlic powder

- 1 teaspoon ground coriander seed

- 3 whole cloves

- 7 whole peppercorns

- 4 tomatoes, chopped

- 2 tablespoons plain yogurt

Direction

- In a big skillet, heat oil over medium heat; sauté the onion for 5 minutes till golden.

- Put yogurt, tomatoes, peppercorns, cloves, coriander, garlic powder, turmeric, chili powder, water, salt and zucchini and combine all together. Turn the heat to low and allow to simmer for 10 minutes, mixing from time to time.

Nutrition Information

- Calories: 231 calories;

- Sodium: 705

- Total Carbohydrate: 24.4

- Cholesterol: 1

- Protein: 5.7

- Total Fat: 14.4

Spicy Vietnamese Quick Pickled Vegetables

Serving: 10

Ingredients

- 1/2 pound carrots, peeled and cut into matchsticks

- 1/2 pound purple daikon radish, peeled and cut into matchsticks

- 1/2 pound English cucumber, sliced into thin rounds

- 2 jalapeno peppers, sliced into rings

- 2 cups water

- 1 1/2 cups rice vinegar

- 2 tablespoons white sugar

- 2 teaspoons salt

Direction

- Examine 2 mason jars for cracks and rings for rust, get rid of any damaged ones. Submerge in simmering water till vegetables are ready. Use warm soapy water to rinse new, unused rings and lids.

- Distribute jalapeno peppers, cucumbers, radishes and carrots equally between 2 clean jars.

- In a medium saucepan, mix salt, sugar, vinegar and water together. Boil and cook for 3 minutes till sugar has dissolved. Switch heat off and allow to cool for 2 minutes. Put mixture on top of vegetables in jars and allow to come to room temperature, about half an hour.

- Screw on lids and chill for a minimum of 1 hour prior to serving.

Nutrition Information

- Calories: 27 calories;

- Total Carbohydrate: 6.3

- Cholesterol: 0

- Total Fat: 0.1

- Protein: 0.7

- Sodium: 487

Spinach With Chickpeas And Fresh Dill

Serving: 6

Ingredients

- 2 tablespoons olive oil

- 1 large onion, thinly sliced

- 1 1/2 cups canned chickpeas, drained

- 1 pound spinach

- 1/2 cup minced fresh dill weed

- 2 lemons, juiced

- salt and pepper to taste

Direction

- Heat olive oil in a big skillet over medium heat. Put in onion then sauté until it becomes soft. Put in chickpeas then toss to coat with oil.

- Clean the spinach well and remove thick stems. Put undrained spinach and dill into the skillet. Cook until it becomes tender.

- Mix in lemon juice. Season it with pepper and salt to taste. Serve while warm.

Nutrition Information

- Calories: 142 calories;

- Cholesterol: 0

- Protein: 6.6

- Total Fat: 6

- Sodium: 163

- Total Carbohydrate: 20.3

Spinach Stuffed Butternut Squash Patties

Serving: 14

Ingredients

1 butternut squash - peeled, halved, seeded, and grated

1 potato, peeled and grated

1/2 onion, peeled and grated

1 teaspoon salt, or to taste

1/2 cup all-purpose flour

1 egg

1/2 teaspoon ground black pepper

1/2 teaspoon baking powder

3 tablespoons olive oil, divided

4 cups chopped fresh spinach

Direction

In a big bowl, mix together salt, onion, potato and butternut squash; let rest for 10 minutes till moisture is released. Move to a colander and squeeze out excess moisture.

In a bowl, put squash mixture and stir in baking powder, black pepper, egg and flour till well incorporated.

In a skillet over medium heat, heat a tablespoon olive oil; cook while stirring spinach for 2 minutes till wilted. Put in pepper and salt to season spinach; move to a bowl.

Spoon approximately 1 1/2 tablespoons squash mixture and use hands to shape into a small ball; pat into a patty. Put a teaspoon spinach into the patted patty and shape patty surrounding spinach into a ball. Pat the ball with your palms. Redo with the rest of squash mixture and spinach, making 12 to 14 additional spinach-stuffed patties.

In a big skillet over medium heat, heat a tablespoon olive oil; cook patties for 4 to 5 minutes on each side till lightly browned. Put cooked patties into a plate, and redo with the rest of oil and patties.

Nutrition Information

Calories: 97 calories;

Total Fat: 3.4

Sodium: 200

Total Carbohydrate: 15.8

Cholesterol: 13

Protein: 2.3

Spiralized Brown Butter Sage Sweet Potato

Serving: 4

Ingredients

1 large sweet potato, peeled and halved crosswise

1 tablespoon olive oil, or more as needed

1/4 cup butter

9 fresh sage leaves

salt to taste

Direction

Use a spiralizer to slice the sweet potato into ribbons like spaghetti.

In a big nonstick frying pan, heat oil on medium. Add the ribbons of sweet potato; stir frequently, add additional oil to keep them from sticking, and cook for 6-7 minutes until they begin to soften. Move to a platter.

In the same frying pan, heat butter until foaming and melted, 1 minute. Add the sage leaves; stir for 2-3 minutes until the leaves are dark green and crisp and the butter turns a rich caramel color. Take the sage leaves out of the butter. Add the sweet potatoes; mix well to coat.

Use salt to season sweet potatoes and crisp sage leaves to garnish.

Nutrition Information

- Calories: 231 calories;
- Sodium: 183
- Total Carbohydrate: 23
- Cholesterol: 31
- Protein: 1.9
- Total Fat: 15

Sweet Potato Gnudi With Sage Butter

Serving: 8

Ingredients

2 sweet potatoes

2 egg yolks

1 cup ricotta cheese

3/4 cup finely shredded Parmigiano-Reggiano cheese

1 teaspoon salt

1/4 teaspoon ground black pepper

1/2 teaspoon ground nutmeg

1/2 cup all-purpose flour, or more as needed

1/2 cup semolina flour, or more as needed

1/2 cup unsalted butter

10 whole fresh sage leaves

1 tablespoon chopped fresh sage leaves

2 tablespoons shredded Parmigiano-Reggiano cheese, or
to taste

Direction

Preheat the oven to 200°C or 400°F.

In the preheated oven, roast sweet potatoes for about an
hour till soft; put aside till cool enough to touch.

Slice cooled sweet potatoes in half lengthwise and scrape
flesh from peels using scoop. Throw potato skin away. On
a work surface, crush flesh of sweet potato; let to rest for
half an hour minimum to release moisture and allow to
cool.

In a bowl, put crushed sweet potatoes and blend with 3/4
cup Parmigiano-Reggiano cheese, ricotta cheese and egg
yolks. Mix in nutmeg, black pepper and salt. Into sweet
potato mixture, slowly put flour till dough pulls together.
Begin with a quarter cup of each all-purpose flour and
semolina flour, putting additional if needed.

Scoop the dough by teaspoonful and roll to make marble-
size balls. Generously drizzle semolina flour, then onto the
prepped baking sheet, put the gnudi. Chill for an hour to
overnight for the best texture.

Boil a big pot of salted water. Turn heat to low and allow the water to simmer. Into the simmering water, slowly drop gnudi, approximately 12 at a time; allow to cook for about 4 minutes till they float to the surface. Let simmer for 4 minutes longer and take off using a slotted spoon. Retain warmth of boiled gnudi while finishing cooking the rest of the batches.

In a big skillet, melt the butter over medium heat and let whole sage leaves cook for about 2 minutes till they are starting to brown and wilt; take off leaves. Leave butter in the skillet. Into the hot butter, mix chopped sage and let cook for about 2 minutes till butter starts to brown and release a nutty aroma. Into the butter, slowly stir the sage and gnudi till gnudi are coated. Use whole leaves of sage to garnish; drizzle 2 tablespoons Parmigiano-Reggiano cheese on top. Serve.

Nutrition Information

Calories: 273 calories;

Total Carbohydrate: 27.2

Cholesterol: 88

Protein: 7.2

Total Fat: 15.3

Sodium: 482

Sweet Potato Latkes

Serving: 8

Ingredients

- 2 sweet potatoes, peeled and shredded

- 2 eggs, lightly beaten

- 1 tablespoon brown sugar

- 2 tablespoons all-purpose flour

- 2 teaspoons ground cloves

- 2 teaspoons ground cinnamon

- 1/4 cup vegetable oil for frying

Direction

- In a colander, put the sweet potatoes. Put a cheesecloth on top of potatoes; squeeze potatoes to release as much juice as can be. To release more liquid, allow the potatoes to sit, then squeeze once more.

- Mix cinnamon, cloves, flour, brown sugar, eggs and sweet potatoes in a big bowl; combine thoroughly.

- In big heavy skillet, heat oil to 190°C or 375°F.

- Shape mixture into pancake size cakes, then fry in hot oil. Turn cakes 2 to 3 minutes after, once bottom turns browned; brown the other side. Let to drain on paper towels then serve while piping hot.

Nutrition Information

- Calories: 68 calories;

- Total Fat: 2

- Sodium: 37

- Total Carbohydrate: 10.6

- Cholesterol: 46

- Protein: 2.3

Sweet Potato And Date Casserole

Serving: 6

Ingredients

- cooking spray

- 2 cups mashed sweet potatoes

- 1 cup pitted, chopped dates

- 3/4 cup brown sugar

- 2 eggs, beaten

- 1/2 cup butter, melted

- 1/2 cup heavy whipping cream

- 1 teaspoon vanilla extract

- 1/2 teaspoon ground cinnamon

- 1/2 teaspoon ground nutmeg

- 1 cup granola cereal

- 1/2 cup brown sugar

- 1/2 cup chopped pecans

- 1/3 cup all-purpose flour

- 1/3 cup butter, melted

Direction

- Preheat the oven to 220 °C or 425 °F. Use cooking spray to coat a 2-quart baking dish.

- In a bowl, mix together nutmeg, cinnamon, vanilla extract, cream, 1/2 cup melted butter, eggs, 3/4 cup brown sugar, dates and sweet potatoes till well incorporated. Scatter mixture into the prepped baking dish.

- In the prepped oven, bake for 20 minutes till hot.

- In a bowl, combine flour, pecans, 1/2 cup brown sugar and granola cereal till mixture is crumbly; put 1/3 cup melted butter into the granola mixture, and mix to incorporate. Scatter granola topping on top of sweet potatoes.

- Bake for 15 minutes longer till topping is slightly golden brown.

Nutrition Information

- Calories: 780 calories;

- Sodium: 291

- Total Carbohydrate: 86.2

- Cholesterol: 157

- Protein: 9.7

- Total Fat: 46.5

Sweet Potatoes With Feta Cheese

Serving: 4

Ingredients

- 2 large sweet potatoes, peeled and sliced

- 1 (4 ounce) package tomato basil feta cheese

- 1 tablespoon balsamic vinegar

Direction

Into a microwave safe dish, put sweet potatoes slices. Pour just enough water to cover. Let cook in the microwave for 10 minutes, or till beginning to become soft.

Preheat an oven's broiler. Onto an oiled broiler pan, put the sweet potato slices. Cut feta cheese the best that you can; put a piece over of every potato slice. Sprinkle balsamic vinegar all over.

Put below the preheated broiler for approximately 6 minutes, or till cheese is browned lightly.

Sweet And Nutty Moroccan Couscous

Serving: 6

Ingredients

- 2 cups vegetable broth

- 5 tablespoons unsalted butter

- 1/3 cup chopped dates

- 1/3 cup chopped dried apricots

- 1/3 cup golden raisins

- 2 cups dry couscous

- 3 teaspoons ground cinnamon

- 1/2 cup slivered almonds, toasted

Direction

- In a large saucepan, boil vegetable broth. Add the apricots, dates, raisins, and butter. Boil the mixture for 2-3 minutes. Remove it from the heat. Mix in couscous. Cover the pan and let it stand for 5 minutes. Mix in toasted almonds and cinnamon; serve.

Nutrition Information

- Calories: 442 calories;

- Total Fat: 14.8

- Sodium: 164

- Total Carbohydrate: 68.2

- Cholesterol: 25

- Protein: 10.5

Thai Charred Eggplant With Tofu

Serving: 4

Ingredients

- 5 small eggplants

- 3 fresh green chile peppers

- 4 cloves garlic, peeled

- 1 tablespoon chopped fresh cilantro

- 1 small onion, quartered

- 3 teaspoons light brown sugar

- 2 tablespoons lime juice

- 1 tablespoon vegetable oil

- 8 ounces tofu, diced

- 1/2 cup chopped fresh basil

Direction

- Preheat a grill to high heat.

- Oil grill grate. Cook eggplants on all sides for 15 minutes or till black and charred. Take off heat. Put on wire rack; cool. Peel then diagonally slice; put aside.

- In blender/food processor, process lime juice, sugar, onion, cilantro, garlic and chile peppers till smooth.

- In a big skillet, heat oil on high heat. Add Chile mixture. Lower heat to medium. Cook it for a minute. Mix in eggplant, 1/4 cup basil and tofu gently. Cook till heated through. Put into serving dish. Use leftover basil as a garnish.

Nutrition Information

- Calories: 219 calories;

- Total Fat: 7

- Sodium: 21

- Total Carbohydrate: 35.5

The Best Steamed Asparagus

Serving: 4

Ingredients

- 1 pound fresh asparagus spears, trimmed

- 1/4 cup white wine

- 2 tablespoons butter

Direction

- In a microwave-safe dish, place asparagus; dot with butter pieces and add wine.

- Cover dish loosely and place in the microwave; cook for 3 minutes on high power or until asparagus becomes tender and bright green in color. Let stand for 5 minutes before serving.

Nutrition Information

- Calories: 86 calories;

- Total Fat: 5.9

- Sodium: 44

- Total Carbohydrate: 4.8

- Cholesterol: 15

- Protein: 2.6

The Very Best Family Style Oyster Dressing

Serving: 12

Ingredients

1 (8.5 ounce) package corn muffin mix

1 egg

1/3 cup milk

1 (8 ounce) box buttermilk biscuit mix

1/2 cup water

1/2 cup unsalted butter, divided

1 onion, chopped

1 cup chicken livers, rinsed and trimmed

1 (14 ounce) package dry herb-seasoned stuffing mix

1 1/2 cups water

1 (12 ounce) jar turkey gravy

2 cups turkey broth, or as desired

1 teaspoon crumbled dried sage

1 tablespoon crushed dried thyme leaves

salt and pepper to taste

2 cups shucked oysters with their liquor

Direction

- Preheat oven to 200°C/400°F then grease 8 muffin cups.

- Beat milk, egg and corn muffin mix till moist in bowl; batter will be a bit lumpy. Rest batter for 3-4 minutes; mix again. Put batter in prepped muffin cups, filling the cups halfway.

- In preheated oven, bake for 15-20 minutes till muffins rise and are golden brown. An inserted toothpick in middle of muffin should exit clean. Remove muffins; cool. Crumble muffins coarsely in very big bowl.

- Bring up oven heat to 230°C/450°F>

- Put biscuit mix in bowl; mix 1/2 cup water in lightly to create soft dough. Turn out dough to floured work surface; knead 2-3 times gently.

Pat dough to 1/2-in. thick. Cut biscuit dough to rounds with 2-in. floured cutter. Put biscuits on ungreased baking sheet.

- Bake biscuits for about 10 minutes in 450° oven till lightly golden brown. Remove biscuits; cool on rack. Crumble biscuits coarsely in bowl with muffin crumbs.

- Lower oven heat to 175°C/350°F then grease 11x15-in. baking dish.

- Melt 1/4 cup unsalted butter in big skillet; mix and cook chicken livers and onion in butter for about 10 minutes till chicken livers aren't pink and onion is translucent. Press fork into chicken livers to mash while cooking. Take off heat; put aside.

- Put herb stuffing mix in big bowl with crumbs. Melt leftover 1/4 cup butter with 1 1/2 cup water in saucepan on medium heat; empty herb packet in saucepan and boil if stuffing mix has a separate packet of herbs. Put mixture on crumbs and dry stuffing mix.

- Put turkey gravy in; mix cooked chicken livers in with butter and onions. Start mixing turkey broth in with big wooden spoon till stuffing is moist yet not soggy. Mix black pepper, salt, thyme and sage in; spoon dressing lightly into prepped baking sheet.

- In preheated oven, bake for 20 minutes; take out of oven. Mix oysters and their juices in gently. Cook for 15 more minutes. Cook for 10 minutes after mixing oysters in if you need to hold stuffing for short while. Remove from the oven; use aluminum foil to cover dish. Serve immediately.

Nutrition Information

- Calories: 443 calories;

- Total Fat: 14.6

- Sodium: 1163

- Total Carbohydrate: 58

- Cholesterol: 134

- Protein: 18.9

Three Pepper Pilaf

Serving: 4

Ingredients

4 skinless chicken thighs

3 cups chicken stock

1 onion, chopped

3 cloves garlic, chopped

1 teaspoon ground turmeric

4 ounces fresh mushrooms, sliced

12 ounces uncooked white rice

3 tomatoes, sliced

1 red bell pepper, sliced

1 green bell pepper, sliced

1 yellow bell pepper, thinly sliced

Direction

- Boil chicken pieces with chicken stock in a big pot, putting garlic and onion into stock prior to boiling. Once chicken is cooked through, take out of stock and reserve. Put in turmeric and mix, then reserve stock.

- Heat oil in a big skillet. Put in mushrooms and sauté for a minute. Put in rice, mix for 2 minutes, then put in stock. Simmer gently for 20 minutes. Meanwhile, peel and cut tomatoes and put into the pilaf mixture. Slice the cooked chicken into bite size portions, and put into skillet, together with the yellow, green and red bell peppers. Mix everything together and simmer over low heat, mixing, till all liquid is soaked up and rice is fluffy and separate.

Nutrition Information

- Calories: 467 calories;

- Total Fat: 4.4

- Sodium: 551

- Total Carbohydrate: 83.1

- Cholesterol: 58

- Protein: 23.3

Truffled Mashed Sweet Potatoes

Serving: 6

Ingredients

- 3 large sweet potatoes, peeled and chopped

- 3 tablespoons butter

- 2 tablespoons chicken bouillon granules

- 1 tablespoon ground black pepper

- 1 1/2 teaspoons white truffle oil

- 1 teaspoon garlic powder

Direction

- Boil a big pot of water; put sweet potatoes and allow to cook for 15 minutes till soft. Let the water drain and put sweet potatoes back into the pot; mash till smooth. Mix in garlic powder, truffle oil, black pepper, chicken bouillon granules and butter till smooth.

Nutrition Information

- Calories: 266 calories;

- Total Fat: 7.4

- Sodium: 541

- Total Carbohydrate: 47.1

- Cholesterol: 16

- Protein: 4.2

Ukrainian Filled Halushky Dumplings

Serving: 4 | Prep: 30mins | Cook: 2hours40mins |
Ready in:

Ingredients

- 2 cups shredded potatoes, drained and pressed

- 1 cup cold mashed potatoes

- 1 egg, beaten

- 1 teaspoon grated onion

- salt and ground black pepper to taste

- 3/4 cup all-purpose flour

- 2 teaspoons baking powder

- 2 cups dry cottage cheese

- 1 egg, beaten

- 1 pinch salt

Direction

- Boil a big pot of lightly salted water.

- Mix together the onion, egg, mashed potatoes and shredded potatoes in a medium bowl till well incorporated. Season to taste with pepper and salt. Mix baking powder and flour; mix into the potato mixture. Mixture should be thick enough to shape into rounds.

- In a blender or food processor, blend cottage cheese, or strain through a sieve. Mix in salt and egg. Flatten the dough rounds and put 1 teaspoon of filling into the middle. Press the dough surrounding the filling to secure it in.

- Into rapidly boiling salted water, put the halushky, slowly mix one time, and let cook from 5 to 8 minutes. Take off to a colander and let drain. Put in a serving platter, liberally scatter browned butter on top, and toss gently. Serve along with sour cream.

Nutrition Information

- Calories: 310 calories;

- Protein: 23.9

- Total Fat: 2.8

- Sodium: 395

- Total Carbohydrate: 47.2

- Cholesterol: 103

Vegetable And Feta Latkes

Serving: 6

Ingredients

- 2 1/2 cups grated zucchini

- 1 cup peeled and shredded potatoes

- 1 cup shredded carrots

- 1/2 teaspoon salt

- 3 eggs, lightly beaten

- salt to taste

- freshly ground black pepper

- 3/4 cup matzo meal

- 1/2 cup chopped fresh parsley

- 1/2 cup crumbled feta cheese

- 1/4 cup vegetable oil

Direction

- In a colander, put carrots, potato and zucchini, set a cheesecloth or paper towels over the top and squeeze out as much moisture as you can. Scatter salt on top of vegetables and allow to drain for 15 minutes. Squeeze vegetable once more time in paper towels.

- Mix together pepper, salt, vegetables and eggs in a big mixing bowl. Combine thoroughly. Mix in feta, parsley and flour or matzo meal.

- In a big frying pan, heat vegetable oil. Put the vegetable mixture shaped into pancake sized cakes in hot oil and fry till golden brown on every side, about 2 to 3 minutes on each side. Put in additional oil as necessary to keep cakes frying up well. Drain fried latkes on paper towels.

Nutrition Information

- Calories: 224 calories;
- Total Fat: 14.6

- Sodium: 390

- Total Carbohydrate: 17.3

- Cholesterol: 104

- Protein: 7.6

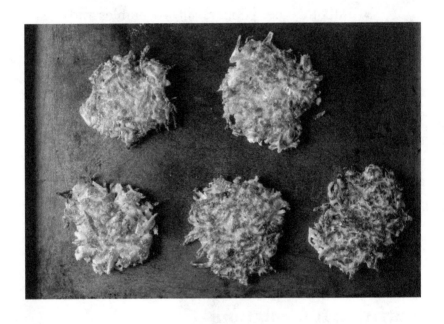

Wild Mushroom Stuffing

Ingredients

- 2 cups hot water

- 1 ounce dried porcini mushrooms

- 1 3/4 pounds egg bread, crust trimmed

- 6 tablespoons unsalted butter

- 4 cups coarsely chopped leeks

- 1 cup shallots, chopped

- 1 1/4 pounds crimini mushrooms, sliced

- 1/2 pound fresh sliced shiitake mushrooms

- 2 cups chopped celery

- 1 cup chopped fresh parsley

- 1 cup chopped toasted hazelnuts

- 3 tablespoons chopped fresh thyme

- 2 tablespoons chopped fresh sage

- 2 eggs

- 3/4 cup chicken stock

- salt to taste

- ground black pepper to taste

- 1 cup dried porcini mushrooms

Direction

- Mix porcini mushrooms and 2 cups of hot water, let sit till mushrooms are tender. Approximately half an hour. Allow to drain, setting aside soaking water. Press porcini to dry and roughly chop.

- Preheat the oven to 165°C or 325°F. Among 2 baking sheets, distribute cubed bread. Bake till starting to brown. Approximately 15 minutes. Let cool then put to a huge bowl.

- In a heavy Dutch oven, liquify butter over medium-high heat. Put shiitake mushrooms, crimini or button, shallots and leeks. Sauté for 15 minutes till soft and golden. Add in porcini mushrooms and celery and sauté for 5 minutes more. To the bowl with the bread crumbs, put the mixture. Add in sage, thyme, hazelnuts and parsley. Put pepper and salt to season and mix in the beaten eggs.

- To bake stuffing in a turkey: with the stuffing, stuff the primary cavity. In a big glass measuring cup, mix half cup of the saved porcini soaking liquid and broth. To the leftover stuffing, put sufficient broth mixture to moisten. Into a buttered baking dish, scoop the leftover stuffing. Cover using a buttered foil. Let stuffing bake in a dish together with turkey for half an hour till heated through. Remove the cover and let bake for 15 minutes till top is crisp.

- To bake every stuffing in pan: preheat an oven to 325°F. Grease a baking dish, 15x10x2-inch in size with butter. Add 3/4 cup of broth and 3/4 cup of saved porcini soaking liquid into the stuffing. Put into the prepped dish. Cover using a buttered foil and let bake for an hour till heated through. Remove the cover and bake for 15 minutes till top is crisp.

Nutrition Information

Calories: 969 calories;

Sodium: 938

Total Carbohydrate: 116.5

Cholesterol: 192

Protein: 37.5

Total Fat: 40.8

Zucchini, Wild Rice, And Hazelnut Fritters

Serving: 8

Ingredients

2 cups water

1/2 cup wild rice

2 zucchini, grated

1 teaspoon salt

1 cup soft bread crumbs

1/2 onion, minced

1/2 cup chopped toasted hazelnuts

2 eggs

1/4 cup whole milk

1 teaspoon baking soda (optional)

2 extra-virgin olive oil, or more as needed

salt and coarsely ground black pepper to taste

Direction

In a small saucepan, boil wild rice and water. Turn heat down to medium-low, put on a cover, and simmer for half an hour till rice is soft. Drain off excess liquid. Allow the rice to cool to room temperature.

In a sieve, toss zucchini along with a teaspoon salt; drain for 10 minutes till liquid is released. Squeeze out excess liquid and move zucchini to a bowl. Stir hazelnuts, onion, bread crumbs and wild rice into zucchini.

In another bowl, beat baking soda, milk and eggs together till incorporated. Stir the egg mixture into zucchini mixture till batter is wet yet not runny.

In a skillet, heat olive oil over medium heat. Spoon batter into hot oil, approximately 2 tablespoons for each fritter. Using a spatula, flatten fritter and cook for 3 to 4 minutes on each side till golden brown. In a plate lined with paper towel, put the fritters to drain; add pepper and salt to season.

Nutrition Information

Calories: 141 calories;

Sodium: 534

Total Carbohydrate: 15.2

Cholesterol: 47

Protein: 5.7

Total Fat: 7.1

THANK YOU

Thank you for choosing *Healthy Recipes for Beginners Quick and Easy* for improving your cooking skills! I hope you enjoyed making the recipes as much as tasting them! If you're interested in learning new recipes and new meals to cook, go and check out the other books of the series.

CPSIA information can be obtained
at www.ICGtesting.com
Printed in the USA
BVHW041734260321
603512BV00014B/1851